GEORGIA

The Peach State

BY
JOHN HAMILTON

Abdo & Daughters
An imprint of Abdo Publishing | abdopublishing.com

abdopublishing.com

Published by ABDO Publishing, a division of ABDO, PO Box 398166, Minneapolis, Minnesota 55439. Copyright © 2017 by Abdo Consulting Group, Inc. International copyrights reserved in all countries. No part of this book may be reproduced in any form without written permission from the publisher. ABDO & Daughters™ is a trademark and logo of ABDO Publishing.

Printed in the United States of America, North Mankato, Minnesota.
012016
092016

THIS BOOK CONTAINS
RECYCLED MATERIALS

Editor: Sue Hamilton   **Contributing Editor:** Bridget O'Brien
Graphic Design: Sue Hamilton
Cover Art Direction: Candice Keimig   **Cover Photo Selection:** Neil Klinepier
Cover Photo: iStock
Interior Images: Alamy, AP, Atlanta Braves, Atlanta Falcons, Atlanta United FC, Center for Civil and Human Rights, Coca-Cola Company, Corbis, Dreamstime, Florida State Archives, Georgia Aquarium, Georgia Port Authority, Getty, Granger Collection, History in Full Color-Restoration/Colorization, iStock, Library of Congress, Mile High Maps, One Mile Up, Robert Lindneux, Science Source, The Masters, U.S. Dept of Agriculture, U.S. Fish & Wildlife Service, U.S. Government.

Statistics: *State and City Populations*, U.S. Census Bureau, July 1, 2014 estimates; *Land and Water Area*, U.S. Census Bureau, 2010 Census, MAF/TIGER database; *State Temperature Extremes*, NOAA National Climatic Data Center; *Climatology and Average Annual Precipitation*, NOAA National Climatic Data Center, 1980-2015 statewide averages; *State Highest and Lowest Points*, NOAA National Geodetic Survey.

Websites: To learn more about the United States, visit booklinks.abdopublishing.com. These links are routinely monitored and updated to provide the most current information available.

Cataloging-in-Publication Data

Names: Hamilton, John, 1959- author.
Title: Georgia / by John Hamilton.
Description: Minneapolis, MN : Abdo Publishing, [2016] | The United States of America | Includes index.
Identifiers: LCCN 2015957510 | ISBN 9781680783124 (print) | ISBN 9781680774160 (ebook)
Subjects: LCSH: Georgia--Juvenile literature.
Classification: DDC 975.8--dc23
LC record available at http://lccn.loc.gov/2015957510

CONTENTS

THE PEACH STATE

Georgia once had a reputation as a slow-paced state where most people worked on farms. Today, it is a state transformed. Southern charm goes hand-in-hand with modern living. Corporations have flocked to Georgia because of its bustling cities and hard-working people.

Georgia is a land of contrasts. Banks, airlines, and telecommunications companies dominate fast-growing Atlanta, while in coastal Savannah a slower pace of life is the norm. Most people live in urban areas, but Georgia's natural beauty and wide-open spaces are treasured.

Though not as important today, agriculture is still a big part of Georgia's economy. Many products are produced here, but the state is most famous for its juicy peaches. Georgia is called "The Peach State" because the fruit thrives in the state's rich soil and moderate climate.

Centennial Olympic Park in Atlanta, Georgia.

Forsythe Park in Savannah, Georgia.

QUICK FACTS

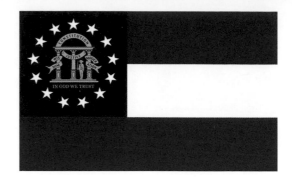

Name: Georgia is named after Great Britain's King George II. He reigned from 1727 to 1760.

State Capital: Atlanta, population 456,002

Date of Statehood: January 2, 1788 (4th state)

Population: 10,097,343 (8th-most populous state)

Area (Total Land and Water): 59,425 square miles (153,910 sq km), 24th-largest state

Largest City: Atlanta, population 456,002

Nickname: The Peach State

Motto: Wisdom, Justice, and Moderation

State Bird: Brown Thrasher

State Flower: Cherokee Rose

Quartz

State Gemstone: Quartz

State Tree: Live Oak

State Song: "Georgia On My Mind"

Live Oak

Highest Point: Brasstown Bald, 4,784 feet (1,458 m)

Lowest Point: Atlantic Ocean, 0 feet (0 m)

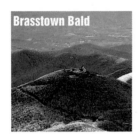

Brasstown Bald

Average July High Temperature: 91°F (33°C)

Record High Temperature: 112°F (44°C), in Louisville on July 24, 1952, and Greenville on August 20, 1983

Average January Low Temperature: 35°F (2°C)

Record Low Temperature: -17°F (-27°C), at CCC Fire Camp F-16, in Floyd County, on January 27, 1940

Average Annual Precipitation: 49 inches (124 cm)

Number of U.S. Senators: 2

Jimmy Carter

Number of U.S. Representatives: 14

U.S. Presidents Born in Georgia: Jimmy Carter

U.S. Postal Service Abbreviation: GA

QUICK FACTS

GEOGRAPHY

Georgia is a Southern state. It is the largest state east of the Mississippi River. It is located in the southeastern part of the United States. It shares its northern border with both Tennessee and North Carolina. Northeast of Georgia is South Carolina. To the west is Alabama. To the south is Florida. Georgia's southeastern corner borders the Atlantic Ocean.

Georgia is the 24th-largest state. It covers 59,425 square miles (153,910 sq km). It measures about 298 miles (480 km) from north to south, and 230 miles (370 km) from east to west. The state has three main regions: the mountains of the north, the central Piedmont, and the low coastal plain.

The beautiful Tallulah Gorge is in mountainous northeastern Georgia.

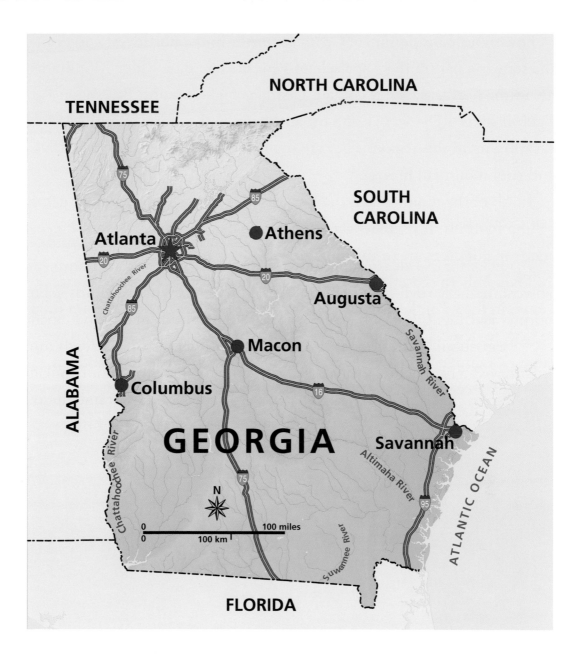

Georgia's total land and water area is 59,425 square miles (153,910 sq km). It is the 24th-largest state. The state capital is Atlanta.

Low mountains dominate Georgia's north. In the northwest corner of the state is a part of the Appalachian Plateau. The Blue Ridge Mountains are in the northeast. They contain Georgia's highest point, Brasstown Bald. It soars 4,784 feet (1,458 m) above sea level. Georgians enjoy vacationing in this region. They are drawn to its many streams, waterfalls, and cool mountain breezes.

South of the mountains is the Piedmont. It is a plateau region of gently rolling foothills. It stretches across the middle of Georgia. Most of the state's major cities are in the Piedmont.

The southern coastal plain is Georgia's largest region. Many crops are grown in these flat, fertile lowlands. In the far southeast, the elevation drops to near sea level. There are many swamps. The Okefenokee Swamp is the largest swamp in North America. Most of it today is protected parkland.

An alligator swims in the Okefenokee Swamp, the largest swamp in North America. The unspoiled wetlands are spread over about 700 square miles (1,813 sq km), mostly in the southeast corner of Georgia.

A wild horse on Cumberland Island National Seashore.

Along Georgia's 100-mile (161-km) Atlantic Ocean coast are many barrier islands. Cumberland Island National Seashore is home to sand dunes, forests, wetlands, and wild horses.

Georgia's most important rivers include the Savannah, Flint, Altamaha, Suwannee, and Chattahoochee Rivers. The Chattahoochee River is the state's longest. It is about 430 miles (692 km) long. The largest body of water is Lake Lanier. It is a reservoir created by a dam on the Chattahoochee River. It provides most of the drinking water for the city of Atlanta.

CLIMATE AND
WEATHER

Georgia's southern coastal plain and Piedmont regions have a humid subtropical climate. Summers are long, hot, and sticky. Winters are mild. In the mountainous northern region, temperatures are more moderate. Summers are still warm, but winters can be cold and snowy. Freezing rain is a common winter hazard in the mountains.

Statewide, Georgia's average July high temperature is 91°F (33°C). In January, the average low is 35°F (2°C). The hottest temperature

A worker wipes sweat on a hot Georgia day.

ever recorded in Georgia is 112°F (44°C). It happened in Louisville on July 24, 1952, and in Greenville on August 20, 1983. The coldest temperature occurred on January 27, 1940, in Floyd County. On that day, the thermometer plunged to -17°F (-27°C).

A lightning storm illuminates the city of Atlanta. According to the National Weather Service, Georgia is the 8th-highest state in terms of density of lightning strikes per square mile.

Georgia normally receives much rainfall across the state. It averages 49 inches (124 cm) of precipitation each year. More rain falls in the mountains of the northeast. Sometimes terrible droughts strike Georgia. Severe thunderstorms often spawn tornadoes, but they are usually small. Hurricanes also sometimes blow in from the Atlantic Ocean.

CLIMATE AND WEATHER

PLANTS AND
ANIMALS

Georgia has many kinds of plants because it has many ecosystems. Wetlands are found in the state's south, and mountain ridges in the north. Unique plants have adapted to these varied environments.

Forests cover more than two-thirds of Georgia. About 250 species of trees grow in the state. One of the most common are red cedar. Found throughout Georgia, these pleasant-smelling trees grow up to 50 feet (15 m) tall and host many species of butterflies. Eastern white pine is found mainly in the northern mountains. Other common trees include palmettos, sugar maples, hickories, cypress, and sweet gum.

An eastern swallowtail butterfly thrives in a garden in Athens, Georgia.

14

GEORGIA

Spanish moss hangs from live oaks lining an avenue leading up to the Wormsloe Historic Site in Savannah, Georgia. The site is a colonial estate once owned by Noble Jones, who arrived in 1733 with the first group of settlers from England.

Georgia's official state tree is the live oak. These large shade trees are usually found along the coast and lower coastal flatlands. They have thick evergreen foliage and strong wood. Their acorns feed many forest animals.

Georgia's state flower is the white-petaled Cherokee rose. The state wildflower is the azalea. Other native Georgia wildflowers include black-eyed Susan, sunflower, swamp milkweed, and blue wild indigo.

PLANTS AND ANIMALS

White-Tailed Deer

White-tailed deer are found in Georgia's woodlands. Their name comes from the white color of the underside of their tails. Georgia is also home to almost 90 other species of mammals. They include opossums, raccoons, gray foxes, gray bats, river otters, bobcats, pygmy shrews, deer mice, swamp rabbits, beavers, muskrats, pocket gophers, and skunks.

Georgia's marine mammals include manatees and dolphins. The North Atlantic right whale is Georgia's official state marine mammal. These endangered animals can weigh up to 100 tons (91 metric tons).

The official state reptile of Georgia is the gopher tortoise. They spend most of their time in their burrows, which can be up to 10 feet

Gopher Tortoise

(3 m) deep. Other reptiles found in Georgia include American alligators, turtles, and skinks. The alligator snapping turtle is the largest freshwater turtle in North America.

Cottonmouth or Water Moccasin Snake

A wide variety of beautifully colored snakes are found all over Georgia. Most are harmless. Poisonous snakes include rattlesnakes, copperheads, and cottonmouths, which are also called water moccasins.

Green Tree Frog

The American green tree frog is the official state amphibian. These small frogs have large toe pads for climbing. They are often seen or heard in backyards in southern Georgia. Other amphibians in the state include bullfrogs and more than 50 kinds of salamanders.

Georgia's official state fish is the largemouth bass. The brown thrasher is the state bird. Honeybees are Georgia's official state insect.

HISTORY

Before Europeans came to the New World, thousands of Native Americans made their home in present-day Georgia. The earliest people settled the land nearly 13,000 years ago. Other early inhabitants included people from the Clovis culture. They were famous for their stone arrowheads and spear tips.

People from the Woodland Period appeared starting around 1000 BC. They were hunter-gatherers who eventually settled in villages and began farming. Some of these people were mound builders. These large, earthen monuments were used in religious ceremonies and as burial places. Many can still be seen today and are preserved as historic parks.

Rock Eagle Effigy Mound is preserved today near Eatonton, Georgia. The 120-foot (37-m) -wide stone bird is believed to have been built by the Woodland Indians 1,000 to 3,000 years ago.

Hernando de Soto and his conquistadors crossed Georgia's Chattahoochee River in 1540. Although the Spanish explorers did not stay in the area, they carried European diseases that Native Americans had no defense against. Many Native Americans died after encountering the Europeans.

By the time European explorers first came to present-day Georgia in the early 1500s, the Native Americans had formed well-organized societies. The two biggest tribes were the Creeks and Cherokees.

Spanish explorers were probably the first Europeans to set foot in Georgia. They did not make serious attempts to permanently settle Georgia. Lucas Vázquez de Ayllón tried to create a settlement in 1526, but it lasted less than two months. Hernando de Soto and his conquistadors traveled through the area in 1540.

HISTORY

Native Americans greet James Oglethorpe and the first English settlers in Savannah, Georgia, in 1733.

Spain and Great Britain struggled for control of Georgia in the late 1600s and early 1700s. In 1733, the land became a British colony. Led by politician James Oglethorpe, 120 British settlers founded the city of Savannah.

Oglethorpe called the new colony Georgia in honor of Great Britain's King George II. Georgia was the last of the 13 American colonies to be established.

At first, the colonists of Georgia were not allowed to own slaves. That changed in 1751. Africans were kidnapped from their homes and brought to Georgia. The slaves were forced to work on plantations that grew cotton, rice, and sugarcane.

Savannah, Georgia, was captured by the British in 1778. Despite efforts by the Americans, the city remained under British control until the war ended in 1783.

In 1776, Georgia joined the other 12 colonies in declaring independence from Great Britain. During the American Revolution, the British captured Savannah in 1778. Great Britain controlled most of Georgia until the war ended in 1783.

After the war, representatives from Georgia signed the U.S. Constitution on January 2, 1788. This made Georgia the fourth state to join the Union.

In the last years of the 1700s, land-hungry settlers began migrating to Georgia. In 1838 and 1839, thousands of Cherokee, Creek, and other Native Americans were forced to move west to Oklahoma. Today, the brutal trek is called the Trail of Tears. The Native American land was turned over to plantation owners, who grew cotton and other cash crops. The plantations used many slaves to harvest the crops cheaply.

The Battle of Atlanta during the Civil War.

In 1861, Georgia joined 10 other Southern states in forming the Confederate States of America. The United States government wanted to abolish slavery, but the Southern economy was too dependent on cheap slave labor to give it up without a fight.

Georgia suffered great destruction during the Civil War. In 1864, Union General William T. Sherman and his soldiers marched through a wide swath of the state. They destroyed everything in their path in what has become known as Sherman's March to the Sea. By the time the war ended in 1865, much of the state was in ruins.

Georgia's recovery after the Civil War was long and painful. There was much economic hardship and political disruption. Eventually, the state began to industrialize and rebuild. By the early 1900s, Georgia was moving away from relying so much on agriculture. Many factories were built. During World War II, new military bases brought jobs and helped the Georgia economy.

Despite these gains, many Georgia citizens continued to face poverty and injustice. Racial violence often gripped the state. In the 1950s and 1960s, Georgia became a home base for civil rights leaders such as Martin Luther King Jr. They fought for equal rights and an end to segregation.

Today's Georgia is a state transformed. A great many of its citizens are prosperous. Its cities, especially Atlanta, are growing fast. Challenges remain, but modern Georgia continues to attract people looking for happiness and opportunity.

Martin Luther King Jr. and his wife Coretta Scott King (center front) lead a civil rights march in Atlanta, Georgia, in 1966.

DID YOU KNOW?

- The Confederate Memorial Carving at Stone Mountain is an immense sculpture near Atlanta. It is the largest high relief carving in the world. It shows three famous Confederate figures from the Civil War: President Jefferson Davis, General Robert E. Lee, and General Thomas J. "Stonewall" Jackson. Completed in 1972, the sculpture measures 90 feet (27 m) by 190 feet (58 m). It is bigger than South Dakota's famed Mount Rushmore.

- Coca-Cola was first sold in 1886, at a soda fountain in Jacob's Pharmacy in Atlanta. It was invented by pharmacist Dr. John Pemberton. At first, the carbonated drink was sold as a medicine. Today, the Coca-Cola Company is one of the largest soft-drink makers in the world. Its headquarters is in Atlanta.

- In almost every state's history, the capital has moved at least once. Georgia has had five capitals. The first capital in colonial times was Savannah. After that came Augusta, Louisville, and Milledgeville, before Atlanta became the current seat of state government.

The ruins of an Atlanta, Georgia, train station in 1864.

- Atlanta's official city symbol is the phoenix, the mythical bird that was burned but then rose to life from the ashes. Most of Atlanta was burned to the ground during the Civil War. Only about 400 buildings survived. That makes Atlanta the only major North American city to be destroyed as an act of war.

- Atlanta rests on the Eastern Continental Divide. Rain that falls to the south and east sides of the divide winds up in rivers that flow into the Atlantic Ocean. However, rain that falls to the north and west flows into the Gulf of Mexico.

- There are more than 55 streets in Atlanta with the name "Peachtree." They may not necessarily refer to peach trees. Some historians say the streets are named after a Creek Native American village called "Standing Pitch Tree." ("Pitch" refers to the sticky sap of pine trees.) The village was located near modern Atlanta's downtown. Over the years, the name has been changed to "Peachtree." Other historians doubt this theory. One thing is for sure: with so many Peachtree Streets, getting directions in Atlanta can sometimes be confusing!

DID YOU KNOW?

PEOPLE

Martin Luther King Jr. (1929-1968) was a civil rights leader of the 1950s and 1960s. Born in Atlanta, he became a Baptist minister at age 25. He believed people should not be judged by their skin color. He organized protests against the injustices many African Americans endured. He condemned violence and insisted on peaceful demonstrations. He was a great public speaker. In 1963, he gave his famous "I Have a Dream" speech in Washington, DC. King's efforts resulted in new laws that helped bring more equality to African Americans. For his civil rights work, he received the Nobel Peace Prize in 1964. Tragically, King was murdered in Memphis, Tennessee, in 1969. King's birthday, January 15, is now a national holiday.

James Earl Carter (1924-) was the 39th president of the United States. He was born in Plains, Georgia. Commonly called "Jimmy," he served in the U.S. Navy and then ran a successful peanut farm in Georgia. Carter was a Democrat who wanted to make government more honest and trusted. He served as president from 1977 to 1981. Before that, he served as the governor of Georgia from 1971 to 1975. He also served in the Georgia State Senate. After serving as president, Carter spent much time doing humanitarian work such as building low-income housing, monitoring elections to make sure they were fair, and fighting diseases in poor countries, especially in Africa. In 2002, Carter was awarded the Nobel Peace Prize.

Ray Charles (1930-2004) was a musician, singer, and songwriter. He was famous for combining rhythm-and-blues music with gospel and jazz, creating a new genre called soul. It influenced early rock-and-roll. Blinded at age seven by the disease glaucoma, Charles learned to read music using braille. He sold millions of records worldwide. In 2004, *Rolling Stone* magazine ranked him as one of the greatest music artists of all time. Charles was born in Albany, Georgia.

Margaret Mitchell (1900-1949) was a journalist and novelist. Her most famous book was *Gone With the Wind*. It was published in 1936. It quickly became one of America's favorite novels. The book takes place in Georgia around the time of the Civil War. It was later made into a movie that won 10 Academy Awards. Mitchell started writing the book because she was bored at home while recovering from a broken ankle. Mitchell was born in Atlanta.

Jackie Robinson (1919-1972) was the first African American to play in Major League Baseball (MLB). Born in Cairo, Georgia, he played many sports as a young man. In 1947, the Brooklyn Dodgers picked him to play first base, breaking the MLB color barrier. Robinson's 10-year career included the MLB Rookie of the Year Award in 1947, a National League Most Valuable Player Award in 1949, six All-Star Game appearances, and a World Series Championship in 1955. He was inducted into the National Baseball Hall of Fame in 1962.

Juliette Gordon Low (1860-1927) founded the Girl Scouts of the United States of America in 1912. She liked to travel and did much charity work. She started the Girl Scouts because she wanted to encourage young women to be caring and self-sufficient, and to help them appreciate sports and the outdoors. She was also the organization's first president. Low was born in Savannah, Georgia.

CITIES

Atlanta is Georgia's largest city and capital. It is sometimes called "The Capital of the South." Its population is 456,002. It is in north-central Georgia, in the Piedmont region. The city was founded in 1837 where two railroad lines came together. At first, the city was called Terminus, then Marthasville, before becoming Atlanta. Burned to the ground during the Civil War, Atlanta has rebuilt and become an economic powerhouse of the 21st century. Including its suburbs, the metro area is home to about four million people. Major industries include food processing, electronics, and communications. Many big corporations are based in Atlanta, including Coca-Cola Company, Delta Air Lines, and Turner Broadcasting System. Atlanta is also home to several universities, including Emory University, Georgia Institute of Technology, and Georgia State University.

Augusta, Georgia's, nickname is the "Garden City of the South" because of its many colorful and large private gardens. The city is located along the Savannah River in east-central Georgia, bordering South Carolina. Its population is 196,741. Established in 1736, is the second-oldest city in Georgia. It was named after Great Britain's Princess Augusta (1719-1772). There are several historic districts in the city, with some homes and buildings dating back to the 1700s. There are also many parks and community centers. Augusta University is an important academic health center with more than 9,000 students. The city is also home to a major golf competition called the Masters Tournament. It is held each year at Augusta National Golf Club.

Columbus is in west-central Georgia, bordering Alabama. It was founded in 1828 on a bluff overlooking the Chattahoochee River. Today, it is a center for textiles, insurance, and many other industries. The U.S. Army's Fort Benning is a major employer. The city boasts many museums and performing arts centers. Its population is 200,887.

Macon is in central Georgia. The city prides itself on its Southern heritage. Its population is 153,691. Manufacturing, agriculture, and medicine are major industries. Many of Macon's historic houses date back to the early 1800s. Ocmulgee National Monument preserves Native American mounds that are more than 1,000 years old.

Savannah is the oldest city in Georgia. Established in 1733, the city today still has many cobblestone streets and ancient live oaks that provide shade. Located in southeastern Georgia where the Savannah River empties into the Atlantic Ocean, the city is a busy seaport. Other industries include food processing, plastics, and airplane manufacturing. Savannah's population is 144,352.

Athens is in the rolling Piedmont region of northeastern Georgia. Its nickname is the "Classic City" because of its many historic landmarks. It is also home to the University of Georgia, the city's largest employer. Poultry and timber are major industries. Athens is famous for its lively music scene and an annual cycling race. The population of Athens is 119,648.

TRANSPORTATION

Hartsfield-Jackson Atlanta International Airport is one of the busiest airports in the world. It handles more passengers than any other airport. More than 250,000 passengers pass through its doors on an average day. Passengers arrive and depart at 191 gates in 6 different concourses. The sprawling airport's grounds contain 5 runways covering 4,700 acres (1,902 ha) of land. The airport handles nearly 1 million flights each year. Besides Atlanta, other major Georgia airports include those in Savannah, Augusta, Columbus, Macon, Athens, Brunswick, Albany, and Valdosta.

Hartsfield-Jackson Atlanta International Airport serves 150 U.S. destinations and more than 75 international destinations in 50 countries. Atlanta is within a two-hour flight of 80 percent of the United States population.

Georgia has more than 128,000 miles (205,996 km) of public roadways crisscrossing the state. Cars, trucks, and busses carry passengers and freight across several major interstate highways. They include I-75, I-20, I-85, I-16, and I-95.

There are two major freight railroads serving Georgia. Passengers can ride on two Amtrak routes.

The Ports of Savannah and Brunswick are major deepwater seaports on the Atlantic Coast. They connect Georgia with cities all across the world, handling bulk cargo such as agricultural products, automobiles, wood, and heavy machinery. Georgia also has two inland ports.

Megaship ZIM Tianjin became the largest container ship to call on the Port of Savannah on March 18, 2015. The ZIM Tianjin, at 1,145 feet (349 m), is nearly as long as New York's Empire State Building is tall.

TRANSPORTATION

NATURAL
RESOURCES

About 65 percent of Georgia's land, or 24.7 million acres (10 million ha) is covered in forest. The state leads the southeastern United States in harvesting timber. Much of Georgia's lumber is pine used to make pulp and paper products.

Almost one-third of Georgia's land area, about 11 million acres (4.5 million ha), is devoted to agriculture. Until the late 1800s, "King Cotton" was the most important cash crop. Today, Georgia's farmers plant a wider variety of crops. Cotton is still important, but it shares Georgia's farm fields with peanuts, pecans, rye, peaches, apples, corn, melons, tomatoes, and many other crops. Georgia grows about 44 percent of all the peanuts consumed in the United States. Georgia is nicknamed "The Peach State" because the juicy fruit thrives in the state's climate and soil.

A farmer near Leesburg, Georgia, harvests his peanut crop. Peanuts are Georgia's official state crop.

Poultry is a very important part of Georgia's agriculture industry. It accounts for about 45 percent of the state's farm income. Beef cattle, dairy cows, and hogs are also raised on Georgia farms.

Georgia ranks number one in mining kaolin, a type of clay used to make china and paper coatings. Other products mined in the state include fuller's earth, granite, limestone, marble, and sand.

On an average day, Georgia poultry farms produce about 29.3 million pounds (13.3 million kg) of broiler chickens, and more than 6.9 million eggs.

NATURAL RESOURCES

INDUSTRY

Manufacturing makes up about 15 percent of Georgia's economy. Its most important products include textiles and clothing, paper products, chemicals, paints, automobiles, electrical equipment, aircraft, glass, and many other items.

Some of America's biggest companies are based in Georgia. They take advantage of the state's educated workforce and positive business climate. Some of the largest companies in Georgia include Home Depot, UPS, Delta Air Lines, Aflac, AT&T Mobility, Rubbermaid, Primerica, and Georgia-Pacific.

Some companies based in Georgia are so big and popular that they are household names. The Coca-Cola Company sold its first drink in Atlanta more than a century ago. The Cartoon Network has been entertaining people with animated programming since 1992. CNN has been producing 24-hour worldwide news coverage in Atlanta since 1980.

The Coca-Cola Company marked its 125th anniversary in May 2011 by using digital projection to illuminate its headquarters in Atlanta, Georgia.

The service industry is also a big part of Georgia's economy. Many business and health service companies are located in the Atlanta area. There are also many banks and financial services companies in the state.

Tourism brings in about $25 billion to the state each year. People vacation in Georgia because of its warm climate, historical sites, fine restaurants and museums, and sporting events.

Georgia locals and tourists enjoy the white sand of Tybee Island's Savannah's Beach.

INDUSTRY

SPORTS

Georgia hosts teams in four major league sports. All are based in Atlanta. The Atlanta Braves is a Major League Baseball team. It moved to Georgia from Milwaukee, Wisconsin, in 1966. One of the team's most famous players was outfielder "Hammerin'" Hank Aaron, who hit 755 home runs during his career.

The National Football League's Atlanta Falcons also started playing in Georgia in 1966. The team has won several division championships. The National Basketball Association's Atlanta Hawks has been playing in Georgia since 1968. Atlanta United FC is a Major League Soccer expansion team.

Professional golf is a popular spectator sport in Georgia. The state's most famous competition is the Masters Tournament, held each year at Augusta National Golf Club. Car racing is also big in Georgia. There are more than 70 speedways and drag strips in the state. In 1996, Atlanta hosted the Summer Olympic Games.

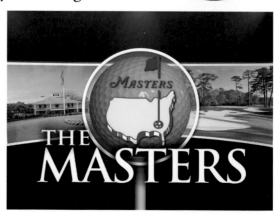

The Masters Tournament is held each year in April in Augusta, Georgia.

In addition to professional sports, Georgians love watching the state's many college teams. There are seven Division 1 teams in Georgia belonging to the National College Athletic Association (NCAA). Many other teams play in other NCAA divisions or collegiate associations.

The Georgia Bulldogs play for the University of Georgia in the city of Athens.

The Georgia Tech Yellow Jackets represent the Georgia Institute of Technology in Atlanta.

The Georgia State Panthers play in Atlanta, Georgia.

The Kennesaw State Owls play in Kennesaw, Georgia.

SPORTS

ENTERTAINMENT

There are many historic sites, fairs, and music festivals throughout Georgia. But the heart of the state's arts and entertainment scene is in Atlanta. This multicultural city boasts many of the best restaurants in the state. It is also home to the Oglethorpe University Museum of Art, the Michael C. Carlos Museum, and the High Museum of Art.

Atlanta's High Museum of Art brings in special exhibits, such as Dutch artist Johannes Vermeer's famous "Girl With a Pearl Earring."

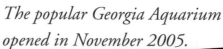

The popular Georgia Aquarium opened in November 2005.

Other Atlanta attractions include the Fox Theater and the Atlanta Opera. The Georgia Aquarium in downtown Atlanta is one of the world's biggest aquariums. It houses thousands of fish and marine mammals, including dolphins and beluga whales. Next door to the aquarium is the World of Coca-Cola, a museum that highlights the history of the Coca-Cola Company. Zoo Atlanta has hundreds of animals, including giant pandas.

Outside of Atlanta, Georgians have many entertainment choices. The Georgia Museum of Art is in Athens. The Morris Museum of Art is in Augusta. There are more than 60 library systems in Georgia, carrying more than 18 million volumes. Georgia is proud of its authors. They include Alice Walker (*The Color Purple*) and Margaret Mitchell (*Gone With the Wind*).

TIMELINE

11,000 BC—The first humans arrive in Georgia. They later group into various Native American tribes.

HERNANDO
DE SOTO

1526—Spanish explorer Lucas Vázquez de Ayllón tries to create a settlement in Georgia, but it lasts only two months.

1540—Spanish explorer Hernando de Soto travels through Georgia.

1733—Spain's claim to Georgia is challenged by England when James Oglethorpe starts a colony at Savannah.

1776—Georgia joins other colonies fighting for independence from Great Britain.

1788—Georgia becomes the fourth state admitted to the United States.

1830s—Native Americans are forced to leave Georgia.

1861—Georgia joins the Confederacy in order to keep slavery legal. The American Civil War begins.

1865—Georgia and all other rebel Southern states are defeated. Slaves are freed.

1886—Dr. John Pemberton creates and sells Coca-Cola in Atlanta, Georgia.

1959—Segregated seating on Atlanta city buses ruled unconstitutional.

1960—Martin Luther King Jr. and others arrested in civil rights sit-in demonstration in Atlanta.

1974—Hank Aaron breaks baseball home run record.

1977—Jimmy Carter is sworn in as the 39th president of the United States.

1996—Atlanta hosts the Summer Olympic Games.

2008—Atlanta-based Delta Air Lines merges with Northwest Airlines to become the world's largest airline.

2014—The Center for Civil and Human Rights opens in Atlanta. The museum highlights American and global civil rights movements.

GLOSSARY

BARRIER ISLAND

Long and narrow landform just offshore from a mainland. Typically made up of sand, silt, or pebbles.

BRAILLE

A type of writing for blind people consisting of patterns of raised dots that are felt with the fingers. It was created in the 1800s by French teacher and inventor Louis Braille (1809-1852), who became blind at age three when playing with a sharp tool at his father's harness shop.

CIVIL RIGHTS MOVEMENT

A nationwide effort beginning in the 1950s to reform federal and state laws so that blacks could enjoy full equality with whites.

CIVIL WAR

The war fought between the Northern and Southern states from 1861-1865. The Southern states were for slavery. They wanted to start their own country. Northern states fought against slavery and a division of the country.

COLONY

A place settled by people from someplace else. Usually, the settlers remain under the control of the government of the place from which they came.

EFFIGY

A sculpture or figure that represents a person or animal.

INDUSTRIALIZE

To change a society or location from one in which work is done mainly by hand to one in which work is done mainly by machines.

NEW WORLD

The areas of North, Central, and South America, as well as islands near these land masses. The term was often used by European explorers.

PIEDMONT

An Italian word that means "at the foot of the hills."

PLAIN

A large, flat area of land. There are few trees on plains. Many plains are filled with grasses.

PLANTATION

A large piece of land in which crops, like cotton, coffee, or tobacco, are raised and harvested by workers who live there.

PLATEAU

A large, flat section of land that is raised up from the surrounding countryside. This area of high ground is mostly flat at the top.

SEGREGATION

To separate things. In many places in the South after the Civil War, African Americans were segregated. They were not allowed to mix with other races in places like restaurants, busses, and schools.

WORLD WAR II

A conflict that was fought from 1939 to 1945, involving countries around the world. The United States entered the war after Japan bombed the American naval base at Pearl Harbor, in Oahu, Hawaii, on December 7, 1941.

INDEX